SPIRIT OF AUSTRALIA

Spectacular panoramic views of Australia

Produced completely in Australia

THANK YOU

I wish to offer my sincere thanks to the sponsors who have endorsed this project as it is only through their support and assistance that we have been able to produce Spirit of Australia as a truly Australian product.

Qantas Airways Limited – from the humble beginnings of a tin shed in outback Queensland to one of the world's leading airlines, Qantas epitomises the Spirit of Australia.

Hanimex / Fuji – there is no better film than Fuji to capture the colours of Australia. Sydney. Phone: 02 938 0400.

Pirie Printers – with a vision to be the preferred supplier of high quality books in Australia, and to reclaim quality printing currently going offshore. Canberra Telephone 06 280 5410.

Spicers Paper Limited – "Committed to keeping printing in Australia." Adelaide, Brisbane, Canberra, Darwin, Hobart, Launceston, Melbourne, Perth, Sydney and Townsville.

Proudly reprinted in Australia by Pirie Printers.
All film processing done by Vision Graphics (Processing) Pty Ltd, Sydney. Phone: 02 929 8658.
Ken Duncan's Limited Edition Prints are produced by Australian Colour Laboratories Pty Ltd, Sydney. Phone: 02 438 3322.
Colour separations produced by Pepcolour Pty Ltd, Brisbane. Phone: 07 865 1911.
To Pamela my beloved wife, I dedicate this book to you.

Renmark Road, Wentworth, New South Wales. ▶

ABOUT THE PHOTOGRAPHER

KEN DUNCAN, one of Australia's most celebrated landscape photographers, has numerous national and international awards to his credit. He is acknow -ledged as one of the world's leading panoramic specialists and his Limited Edition Prints are fetching some of the highest prices received for contemporary photographic works.

He believes the art of photography is in seeing the image. Capturing it on film is the technical craft. He does not see himself as a creator, but rather as an interpreter of God's creation and endeavours to bring this beauty to others so that they may be blessed by it.

The Ken Duncan Gallery just outside Gosford, New South Wales, is one of Australia's leading photographic galleries, where the best of Ken's works are on permanent display.

After the exceptional success of his two previous books, *"The Last Frontier"* and *"Australia Wide"*, the recent registration of Ken Duncan's bold new Trademark **"Panographs"**, derived from *panoramic photographs,* signals a move into publishing for this energetic young photographer. Spirit of Australia is just one title in an exciting new series of Australian produced books featuring Ken Duncan Panographs.

◀ Ken at his camp site, Rainbow Valley, Northern Territory.

Page 1 – Abandoned Homestead, Burra, South Australia.

▲ Mertenally Sand Dunes, Wentworth, New South Wales.

WHAT IS A PANOGRAPH®?

A Panograph is a panoramic photograph, by Ken Duncan, which captures the essence
of a place and a moment in time, to allow the viewer a presence with the image.

Pages 2 & 3 – Crystal Cascades. Cairns, Queensland.

▼ Beach north of Palm Cove, Cairns, Queensland.

INTRODUCTION

SPIRIT OF AUSTRALIA – it is the hidden fibre that flows throughout the nation, holding it together; not for dissection by the hands of knowledge but to be felt by the humble in spirit. For who are we, when we move away from the props of our society and stand beneath the canopy of the stars?

While we are looking inward, we cannot look outward at how awesome creation really is. Are we limited by our knowledge or set free in our spirits to look beyond self and our own circumstances?

Come walk awhile through the freedom and space Australia still has to offer. Leave behind any burdens you bear or preconceptions you have. Come share an adventure of discovery – allow yourself to be absorbed into the scene. Take time, for the world moves on regardless.

Only in stillness can the Spirit begin to touch us and allow us to see more clearly the movement around us.

▼ Lake McKenzie, Fraser Island, Queensland.

We all need a balance in our lives so that we may see ourselves clearly in relationship to the whole of creation. The beauty of God's creation ministers to our spirits; all we need to do is allow it to touch our hearts.

◄ Sunset over the Ocean, Cape Leveque, Western Australia.

▼ God's Marbles, Tennant Creek, Northern Territory.

The Paddle Steamer "Adelaide" on the Murray River, Echuca, Victoria,
is the oldest vessel of its kind still in service in Australia. In early days,
these trusty river boats would carry supplies and news to our pioneer
farmers and return the hard won produce to market.

Butchers Creek, just outside Cloncurry, Queensland,
flowing once again after the summer rains. In rich contrast
to the desolate, scrubby bush for miles around,
the strong river gums cling to their lifeline.

Overleaf – Full Moon rising over the Bungle Bungles, Western Australia.

▲ Tenacious palms cling to the fertile soil of Echidna Chasm, in the Bungle Bungles, Western Australia, awaiting the monsoon rains.

◄ Intriguing clouds form a halo over the world's largest monolith, Uluru, in the heart of the Northern Territory.

Cathedral Rock and Cape Pillar with Tasman Island
in the Background, Tasmania.

Artesian Water flows to the surface near an old Traction
Engine outside Burketown, Queensland.

Wilsons Promontory, the southernmost tip of mainland Australia, is a favourite retreat
for Victorians from the hustle and bustle of city life.

Rich farmland near Maleny, Queensland, with The Glasshouse Mountains
protruding from the fertile plain.

Sailing away is a dream shared by many and scenes like this make the dream even more appealing. Yes, this is the life. Anchored within Hardys Reef, looking down into crystal clear waters teeming with abundant tropical life.

But how many storms has this craft had to weather and how much preparation has gone before this day of glory? Life is full of character building situations and as we face them we break through to our days of rest. ▶

Overleaf – Silent Sentinels, Cape Leveque, Western Australia.

▼ Coral formations in Hardys Reef, Whitsundays, Queensland.

Henty Dunes, just off the road from Strahan to Zeehan,
on the West Coast of Tasmania.

The cool, clear waters of Seventy Five Mile Beach,
Fraser Island, Queensland.

Bell Creek Falls, Isdell River, Silent Grove Station, Western Australia.

The setting sun breaks through stormy clouds upon The Olgas, Northern Territory.

▲ A lightning strike at sea illuminates the night sky.

◄ Thundering waves crash upon the rock shelf, giving this place it's name - Cannonball - on the West Coast of Tasmania.

Overleaf – Twilight on Lake Victoria, New South Wales.

Deloraine Island, Whitsundays, Queensland.

Mitchell Falls, Kimberley, Western Australia.

Ruins of the Kelly Homestead, Glenrowan West, Victoria.

Coolamine Homestead, Kosciusko National Park, New South Wales.

▲ Mist shrouds an Arctic Beech, near Springbrook, Queensland.

◄ Natural Arch, Gold Coast Hinterland, Queensland.

Overleaf – Refuge Cove, Wilsons Promontory, Victoria.

The magic of a rainbow as it splays its hues across the heavens, brings out the child in all of us. Here, in full splendour, the multicoloured arch settles over Sullivans Cove, Hobart, bringing to the scene a seal of mystery. ◀

▼ Rainbow, Hobart, Tasmania.

Maheno Wreck, Fraser Island, Queensland.

Sand Dunes, Indian Head, Fraser Island, Queensland.

▲ Barrenjoey Lighthouse flashes its warning to passing vessels as the sun rises over Palm Beach, New South Wales.

Snow Drift, Cradle Mountain National Park, Tasmania.

Jacarandas in bloom, Dorroughby, New South Wales.

▲ Ghost Gum, Finke River National Park, Northern Territory.

◄ Spectacular King George Falls in Western Australia, plummets 200 feet into the lower reaches of the King George River where salt water crocodiles abound.

Overleaf – Mahon Pool, Maroubra, New South Wales.

Although named "End of the Line", in fact this is the beginning of the line. The early settlers port of Cossack, Western Australia, was abandoned by the townspeople when the water supply could no longer support its population.

While the port still operated, the rail line was used to transport supplies to the new inland town of Roebourne. This railway line was the lifeline to a new start, as the old town was no longer capable of sustaining growth.

So it can be in life when problems occur. When we find we have run dry, do we dwell on the end, or look forward to a new beginning? ▶

Overleaf – Millstream Falls, Atherton Tablelands, Queensland.

▼ Blythe Homestead, Wangi, Northern Territory.

54

Golden Beach, Coffin Bay National Park, South Australia.

Sunset, Freshwater Cove, Wilsons Promontory, Victoria.

Belmore Falls, Morton National Park, New South Wales.

Tree Ferns, Tarra Valley, Victoria.

Overleaf – King Edward River, Mitchell Plateau, Western Australia.

Poinciana Tree in Flower, Mt Garnet, Queensland.

Grass Trees in Bushland outside Perth, Western Australia.

The Grotto, Port Campbell National Park, Victoria.

Blue Haven, Esperance, south coast of Western Australia.

Gone are the days of the hard working cane cutters, for now machinery takes their place. The spirit of hard working men lingers in this abandoned building *(previous page)*. As I spoke with the old farmer, he reminisced about the way the town of Ingham used to be transformed with the arrival of the cutters for the annual harvest. "They would work from before sunrise until after the sun had set. These days," he said, "it's hard enough to get a guy to dig a hole without a machine."

◀ The Pinnacles, Nambung Nat. Park, Cervantes, Western Australia.

▼ Petrol Pump, Silverton, New South Wales.

▲ Twilight glow over rolling hills, near Korumburra, Victoria.

Lake Argyle just outside Kununurra, Western Australia.

An aerial view of the Bungle Bungles, Western Australia.

Most people, including the Northern Territory Government, call these The Devil's Marbles
but I'm endeavouring to have them renamed. That's why I call this formation near
Tennant Creek, Northern Territory, "God's Marbles" and give credit
where credit is due.

Sunflowers are most interesting plants. While they are young and supple their faces follow
the sun's passage through the day. However, as they get older and more stiff necked,
they lose the ability to change. Here a field of young plants
face the rising sun at Mullaley, New South Wales.

"The heavens declare the glory of God; the skies proclaim the work of His hands. Day after day they pour forth speech; night after night they display knowledge. There is no speech or language where their voice is not heard. Their voice goes out into all the earth, their words to the ends of the world.

In the heavens He has pitched a tent for the sun, which is like a bridegroom coming forth from his pavilion, like a champion rejoicing to run his course. It rises at one end of the heavens and makes its circuit to the other; nothing is hidden from its heat."

Psalm 19.

◀ Fisherman at Sunrise, North Avoca, New South Wales.

▼ Shoreline, Avoca Beach, New South Wales.

SPIRIT OF AUSTRALIA
ISBN 0 646 10257 5

Pictures and text: Ken Duncan

© **Ken Duncan**

First printed 1992
Reprinted 1992
2nd reprint 1993
3rd reprint 1994

First published in 1992 by
Ken Duncan Panographs ® Pty Limited
P.O. Box 15, Wamberal NSW 2260 Australia
Phone: 61 43 67 6777

Distributed in Australia by
Peribo Pty Limited
26 Tepko Road, Terrey Hills NSW 2084 Australia
Phone: 02 486 3188

Reprinted 1994, in Australia, by Pirie Printers.

Colour Separations by Pepcolour Pty Limited, Brisbane.
Designed by Trevor Hopgood and Ken Duncan.

Panographs ® is a registered trademark of
Ken Duncan Australia Wide Holdings Pty Ltd.

Other titles in this series:
SPECTACULAR SYDNEY
THE AUSTRALIA WIDE YEARBOOK

Many of the images in this book are available
as signed Limited Edition Photographic Prints.
For further information, contact: Ken Duncan Australia Wide Gallery,
P.O. Box 15, Wamberal NSW 2260. Phone: 61 43 67 6777.